Original title:
The Glimmering Woods

Copyright © 2024 Creative Arts Management OÜ
All rights reserved.

Author: Micah Sterling
ISBN HARDBACK: 978-9916-88-858-2
ISBN PAPERBACK: 978-9916-88-859-9

Shimmering Echoes of a Hidden World

In shadows deep where secrets gleam,
Whispers weave a silent dream.
Among the leaves, a soft refrain,
Echoes drift like drops of rain.

A glint of gold on forest floor,
Nature's treasures, hidden lore.
Each shimmer tells a tale untold,
Of magic wrapped in shades of gold.

The Dance of Dawn's First Light

As sunbeams rise in gentle grace,
They paint the sky, a soft embrace.
Birds awaken, sing their song,
In harmony, where hearts belong.

The world ignites with colors bright,
A symphony of pure delight.
Each dawn's arrival, pure and free,
A dance of hope for you and me.

Whirlwind of Glinting Flora

Petals whirl in vibrant hues,
Dancing lightly to the blues.
In a garden, life does spin,
A whirlwind of joy held within.

Colors clash and softly blend,
Nature's message without end.
Each bloom tells of life's sweet grace,
Whirlwind wonder, a warm embrace.

Threads of Light in a Shady Glade

In the glade where shadows play,
Threads of light keep dark at bay.
Dappled sun on earth below,
Glimmers weave a gentle glow.

Whispers rustle through the trees,
Caressing air, a soothing breeze.
In quietude, the heart finds rest,
Threads of light, nature's best.

Where Sunbeams Meet Mossy Carpets

Sunlight spills on emerald green,
Nature's quilt, a calming scene.
A dance of light on dampened ground,
Whispers of life, a glance profound.

Gentle breezes kiss the leaves,
In this haven, the heart believes.
Patterns weave in golden rays,
Lost in time, where shadows play.

Flickering Glimmers in Mystic Groves

Beneath the boughs, a secret glow,
Where enchanted whispers softly flow.
Fireflies sketch in twilight's hue,
A dance of dreams, both old and new.

Branches sway, a silent song,
In this magic, we belong.
Echoes linger, tales unfold,
In the dark, the light is bold.

Secret Luminosities of Twilight

As the evening softly sighs,
Stars awaken, in the skies.
Shadows drape like whispered sighs,
Painting love beneath the cries.

Crickets chirp their nightly song,
In this wonder, we belong.
The moonlight weaves a silver thread,
Guiding dreams where wishes tread.

The Allure of Sap and Stardust

In the forest, sweet sap flows,
Golden droplets, nature's prose.
Stardust lingers in the air,
Whispers secrets beyond compare.

Trees stand tall with timeless grace,
Guardians of this sacred place.
With every breath, we feel the blend,
Of earth and sky, where wonders mend.

Shining Whispers of Old Growth

In the shadows, secrets dwell,
Among the ancient trees they tell.
Whispers soft as morning dew,
Echo dreams of woodlands true.

Leaves rustle with stories rich,
Time's embrace, a gentle stitch.
Sunlight dapples, golden grace,
Old growth stands, a timeless place.

Roots entwined in silent lore,
Every ring, a journey's core.
Nature breathes in quiet sighs,
Underneath the boundless skies.

In this realm of green and sound,
Life's mosaic is profound.
Shining whispers hold the past,
In their arms, forever cast.

A Lantern's Heart Among the Branches

Amid the boughs, a light does glow,
A lantern's heart, soft and low.
Guiding lost souls through the night,
Casting warmth in silver light.

Through leaves that dance with evening breeze,
It twinkles down with gentle ease.
A beacon in the darkened wood,
A promise kept, where hope once stood.

Stars above begin to peep,
Guardians of the dreams we keep.
In this forest, shadows play,
While the lantern lights the way.

Every flicker, a whispered prayer,
An echo of the heart laid bare.
Bound by love, this light will stay,
A lantern's heart will guide the way.

Petals Adrift in a Shiny Stream

Petals drifting down the flow,
In the current's soft, sweet glow.
Each a whisper, bright and free,
Floating gently, wild as me.

Colors dance on water clear,
Nature's laughter, pure and near.
Soft reflections, skies above,
In this moment, life and love.

Ripples tell of tales untold,
In hidden dreams, the world is bold.
Petals roam where waters gleam,
In the heart of nature's dream.

A journey small, yet vast it seems,
Carried forth on water's beams.
Petals adrift, a tender stream,
Together in a shining dream.

Glistening Journeys in Nature's Heart

In the forest, pathways weave,
Glistening trails for those who believe.
Nature's heart beats strong and true,
With every step, a world anew.

Morning mist, a shrouded veil,
Whispers found in soft detail.
Every leaf a story spun,
In the shade, gives life to fun.

Rivers flow with echoes bright,
Crickets chirp in fading light.
Every journey paints its part,
In the depths of nature's heart.

Beneath the stars, all fears depart,
Adventure calls, a work of art.
Glistening moments, wild and free,
In nature's soul, we find the key.

Dappled Patrons of the Forest Floor

Beneath the trees, shadows play,
Whispers dance in dappled light.
Ferns unfurl in gentle sway,
Nature's creatures take to flight.

Mossy carpets cradle feet,
Secrets held in leafy seams.
Squirrels chatter, quick and fleet,
Awakening the forest's dreams.

Ethereal Glow of the Nature's Heart

In twilight's breath, the world ignites,
Stars emerge from a hushed deep.
Moonbeams cast their silver rites,
Over valleys, where shadows creep.

Flowers bloom in fragrant bliss,
Petals glow with whispers sweet.
Nature's pulse, in every kiss,
Binds the night to life's heartbeat.

Woodland Spectacles in Multicolored Hues

Autumn paints the leaves with flair,
Crimson, gold, and amber bright.
Crisp air carries scents so rare,
Whirling colors, pure delight.

Mushrooms sprout in playful rows,
Hidden gems in earthy beds.
Creatures weave through sunlit glows,
Nature's palette softly spreads.

Embers of Light on Nature's Canvas

Dawn unfurls, a golden brush,
Brushing skies with hues of fire.
Every moment holds a rush,
Nature's song, a sweet desire.

Stars fade into the morning's rise,
Whispers of the night depart.
Each new day brings fresh surprise,
Embers stir within the heart.

A Dreamscape in Silhouette

In shadows cast by the fading light,
Whispers of stars begin their flight.
The night unfolds its velvet embrace,
As dreams take shape in a tranquil space.

Beneath the moon's soft, silver gaze,
Heartbeats sync in a wondrous maze.
Each thought a thread in a cosmic seam,
Woven tight in a timeless dream.

Figures dance in the quiet air,
Ghostly echoes that linger there.
The world dissolves in a gentle sigh,
As shadows play with the night sky.

Awake or asleep, who can tell?
In this realm where illusions dwell.
A dreamscape rich in deep delight,
Silhouettes weave through the endless night.

Hidden Gleams in Nature's Embrace

Among the leaves, a shimmer glows,
Secrets whispered by the wind that flows.
Petals part to disclose the scene,
Nature's canvas, lush and serene.

Sunlight dapples the forest floor,
Creating paths we long to explore.
Each nook holds a truth, pure and bright,
In the heart of day, hidden light.

Rippling streams sing a quiet tune,
Mirroring the warmth of noon.
Underneath the sky so blue,
Magic stirs in the gentlest hue.

Beneath the boughs, life intertwines,
Every creature a part of designs.
Gleams of wonder, nature's grace,
In every corner of this sacred space.

Enigmatic Glow of Mossy Floors

In shadows where the soft moss lies,
A whispering breeze through ancient sighs.
Emerald stories, veiled in green,
Secrets hidden, sights unseen.

The world below, a mystic dream,
Life flows gently like a stream.
Each step reveals a silent lore,
In every fold, a heart to explore.

Glimmering Secrets of the Wild

Beneath the leaves, the echoes play,
Nature's hands weave night and day.
A hidden path where creatures roam,
Every rustle hints of home.

In twilight's arms, the shadows glide,
With secrets deep the woods confide.
Glimmers dance in soft moonbeams,
Carrying forth forgotten dreams.

Light's Dance on Leafy Boughs

Sunlight spills through crowns of trees,
Catching whispers in the breeze.
Leaves shimmer in a golden hue,
Nature's canvas, vivid and true.

Each flutter speaks of joy and grace,
In this enchanted, sacred space.
Light pirouettes, a fleeting glance,
Inviting all to join the dance.

Radiance in the Quiet Grove

Amidst the stillness, beauty blooms,
A gentle hush that softly looms.
Where time stands still, and hearts align,
In each heartbeat, the stars entwine.

This sacred grove, a refuge found,
Woven whispers, a healing sound.
Radiance fills the cool, sweet air,
Promises linger everywhere.

Winged Wishes on Glistening Wings

Beneath the skies where dreams take flight,
Whispers dance in the gentle night.
With wings of hope, we rise and soar,
Chasing wishes to distant shores.

In twilight's glow, our hearts ignite,
Painting starlight, pure and bright.
Each flutter brings a promise new,
A world of magic waits for you.

The Mystery of Shiny Shadows

In the hush of night, shadows play,
Glimmers of light in a surreal sway.
Secrets linger in every nook,
Enticing souls, come take a look.

Silent whispers on silver streams,
Carrying echoes of forgotten dreams.
The moon unveils a hidden truth,
In the depths of age and youth.

Moonlit Pathways Through Green

Through leafy trails where moonlight beams,
Nature speaks in whispered themes.
Guided by the silver glow,
Step by step, we gently flow.

Every turn holds magic's grace,
A symphony in this sacred space.
In the coolness of the night air,
Two hearts wander without a care.

Stars Gathered in the Thicket

In the thicket, stars convene,
Whispers shared in a cosmic scene.
Fireflies join in the gentle weave,
Lighting paths of hopes to believe.

Within the branches, secrets hum,
A melody soft, like a distant drum.
Their twinkle tells of ancient lore,
Inviting us to explore more.

Tides of Sparkling Green

In the embrace of gentle waves,
Emerald fields begin to sway.
Whispers of the ocean's breath,
Carry dreams of yesterday.

Seashells glint like stars at night,
Buried secrets in the foam.
Nature dances, wild and free,
Calling every heart to roam.

Drifting leaves on silver streams,
Reflecting all that life has known.
In this world of vibrant hues,
Every moment's beauty shown.

With each tide, life ebbs and flows,
Nature sings in rhythmic sound.
In sparkling greens and azure blues,
Eternal magic can be found.

The Luster Lurking Within Nature

Beneath the bark, a glow shines bright,
A hidden charm just out of sight.
Colors blend like dreams untold,
Nature's canvas, pure and bold.

Morning dew on petals rest,
Glistening gems in nature's vest.
In the forest's silent sigh,
Lies a truth we can't deny.

Sunbeams break through leafy screens,
Painting gold on emerald greens.
In every rustle, every breeze,
Luster hides beneath the trees.

Let us wander, hearts set free,
Discovering life's artistry.
In the shadows, light will stir,
Nature's whispers are a blur.

Glistening Reflections in Sunlit Spaces

In the morning, sunlight plays,
Dancing on the dew-kissed blades.
Mirrored glints in twilight's charm,
Nature holds us in her arms.

Bubbles rise in sparkling streams,
Each a fragment of our dreams.
Golden light, a gentle guide,
Drawing us to the waterside.

Through the branches, flashes bright,
Painting stories, pure delight.
Every ripple tells a tale,
In the sunlit, sacred vale.

Evening falls, a quiet hush,
Nature's cadence, soft and lush.
In reflections, hearts can find,
Peace unspoken, intertwined.

Ethereal Gleams of Whispering Pines

Among the pines where shadows play,
Ethereal whispers drift and sway.
Soft caresses on the skin,
Nature's symphony begins.

Moonlit paths where secrets dwell,
Each step holds an ancient spell.
Tales of old in breezes flow,
Underneath the stars' soft glow.

Gleams of silver touch the earth,
In this grove, we find rebirth.
Every sigh, a soft embrace,
In the heart of nature's grace.

As the night drapes over all,
Pine trees stand, both proud and tall.
In the stillness, dreams take flight,
Capturing the magic of the night.

A Romance Among Shimmering Blooms

In gardens bright, where flowers bloom,
Two hearts entwined, dispelling gloom.
With whispers soft, they share a dream,
Under the sky, a golden beam.

Petals dance in gentle breeze,
As laughter floats among the trees.
Each glance a spark, a magic thrill,
In love's embrace, the world stands still.

They roam through paths of fragrant hue,
Where every moment feels brand new.
With every kiss, the blossoms sigh,
A romance blooms beneath the sky.

Light Caught in the Web of Nature

Sunlight weaves through leaves so green,
A dazzling glance, a fleeting sheen.
Nature's lace, with shadows played,
In every corner, life displayed.

The brook reflects the sky's embrace,
A silver path, a tranquil space.
Ripples dance with laughter clear,
Echoing the beauty near.

In quiet nooks, the world awakes,
Where light and shadow gently shakes.
A tapestry of sounds and sights,
Captured in nature's pure delights.

Glows of the Verdant Dreamscape

In verdant fields where dreams arise,
A tapestry of emerald lies.
Each blade of grass, a story told,
Beneath the sun, in warmth of gold.

Whispers of the ancient trees,
Carries secrets on the breeze.
With every step, the magic grows,
In hidden paths where wonder flows.

The twilight brings a gentle glow,
As shadows stretch and breezes blow.
A dreamscape rich, alive with schemes,
Where hearts can wander through their dreams.

Shiny Echoes of the Sylvan Realm

In sylvan glades where echoes sing,
The forest whispers, life takes wing.
Glints of light through branches play,
In harmony, the woods convey.

Every creature shares a part,
In nature's song, a beating heart.
The rustle of leaves, a soft refrain,
A melody that knows no pain.

As twilight falls, the stars appear,
Their shimmering glow, a light we steer.
In this realm, where shadows blend,
The echoes of magic never end.

The Enchantment of Light's Embrace

In twilight's glow, the shadows dance,
Cascading beams in soft romance.
Whispers of gold in the cool night air,
A gentle touch, a world laid bare.

The stars awaken, twinkling bright,
Guided by the moon's soft light.
Every corner holds a charm,
In nature's weave, we find our calm.

Through branches high, the light streams down,
Illuminating roots upon the ground.
A fleeting moment, a timeless grace,
Lost in the magic of light's embrace.

Illuminated Paths of Time-Worn Trails

Footsteps echo on the ancient road,
Each stone whispers tales of old.
Through tangled woods, the path unwinds,
A journey etched in hearts and minds.

Sunlight dapples through the leaves,
Painting stories only nature weaves.
Every turn reveals a face,
Of memories held in this sacred space.

As shadows stretch with the setting sun,
The final chapter's just begun.
Time-worn trails beckon us near,
To walk with love, to hold what's dear.

The Radiant Forest Underneath

Beneath the canopy, secrets lie,
In rustling leaves, the softest sigh.
Mossy floors, a verdant sea,
Where flora thrives and spirits flee.

Sunbeams trickle through the trees,
Kissing petals with gentle ease.
Every creature, a hidden light,
Dancing softly in the night.

The vibrant hues of life awake,
Every whisper, a song we make.
A sanctuary of dreams and hope,
In the radiant forest, we learn to cope.

Illuminating the Enchanted Thicket

In tangled greens, a magic glows,
Where fables bloom and wonder grows.
Moonlit paths invite us in,
To weave our tales where dreams begin.

The thicket breathes with ancient lore,
Each rustle hides a world to explore.
In every nook, there's beauty found,
Whispers of the night surround.

Starlit skies weave shadows deep,
Holding close the secrets we keep.
Embraced by night, we find our way,
Illuminated hearts, come what may.

Celestial Reflections on Whispering Streams

Stars twinkle above the glassy flow,
Dreams carried by the gentle current below.
Moonlight dances on the rippling tide,
Whispers of night where our secrets hide.

Silence sings to the heart's deep ache,
Waves embrace the shore, softly awake.
Each thought drifts like leaves in the breeze,
Cradled in shadows of ancient trees.

In the calm, every moment feels vast,
Reflections of futures woven from past.
The stream narrates stories, old and new,
A celestial echo, forever true.

Flickering Fireflies in the Dark

Lights like gems flit in the inky night,
Dancing softly, a mesmerizing sight.
Whispers of magic brush past the trees,
Guides of forgotten tales on the breeze.

Glimmers of hope in the silent woods,
Each flicker a promise, understood.
Celestial sparks in a sea of gloom,
Nature's soft lanterns, lighting the room.

Sweet melodies ripple through the air,
A waltz of shadows with elegance rare.
In the stillness, their glow is a kiss,
Moments enchanted, a fleeting bliss.

Glinting Gems of the Earth

Beneath the soil, treasures lie still,
Shimmering stones, nature's own thrill.
Rivers run deep with secrets untold,
Glinting gems in their embrace, bold.

Each crystal reflects a story of time,
Whispering tales of mountains that climb.
Caves hold the echoes of ages gone by,
In the heart of the earth, secrets lie.

Colors of life in prisms of light,
Mirrors of worlds that dance out of sight.
In every fragment, the universe speaks,
Gems of the earth hold the wisdom we seek.

Melodies of Dappled Sunlight

Sunbeams filter through leaves high above,
Creating a canvas where shadows move.
Notes of nature in harmony play,
Chasing the darkness of lingering grey.

Each burst of light paints the ground gold,
Stories of warmth in the chill of the cold.
Birds sing sweetly, weaving their tune,
In the embrace of the dappled afternoon.

Gentle breezes carry their song far,
Joy in the moment, a bright shining star.
Dappled sunlight, a soothing balm,
In a world of chaos, a moment of calm.

Enchantment Beneath the Bark

Whispers dance on ancient trees,
Secrets held in gentle breeze.
Mossy beds where fairies rest,
Nature's magic, at its best.

Fingers trace the rugged lines,
Stories told in fragrant pines.
Sunlight filters through the green,
Lost in worlds we've never seen.

Captured dreams in wooden shells,
Echoes of forgotten spells.
Every shadow softly twirls,
Enchantment in the hidden curls.

Roots entwined in silent grace,
Time unfolds in this embrace.
Underneath the bark we find,
Mysteries, both sweet and kind.

Reflections in the Dew-Kissed Grasses

Morning breaks on emerald blades,
Glistening like a thousand maids.
Each droplet holds a world anew,
Mirrored sky, in every hue.

Footprints soft upon the trail,
Nature's whisper, a tender tale.
Sunlight weaves through strands so fine,
While the earth begins to shine.

Windsong carries through the field,
Secrets of the day revealed.
Rustling softly beneath our feet,
Where the dew and sunlight meet.

In this moment, time stands still,
Nature's heart, a tranquil thrill.
Reflections spark the soul to sing,
As the day unfurls its wings.

Dreamlike Paradises of the Undergrowth

Mysteries lie where shadows play,
In the thicket, dreams drift away.
Ferns unfold in graceful arcs,
Guiding paths to silent parks.

Mushrooms bloom with colors bright,
Their whispers lost to fading light.
Beneath the boughs, a world takes flight,
Igniting magic, pure delight.

Sunbeams kiss the forest floor,
Nature's breath, an open door.
Wonder weaves through tangled vines,
In this space where the heart aligns.

Every step, a journey bold,
In dreamlike realms, stories unfold.
The undergrowth a timeless clue,
To the wonders waiting for you.

An Odyssey of Luminous Echoes

Stars entwined in velvet night,
Whispers carried on starlit light.
Each echo sings a tale of old,
In the darkness, dreams unfold.

Moonlit paths, we softly tread,
Guided by the light ahead.
Ghostly shadows dance and sway,
In this realm where wishes play.

Celestial seas of shimmering glow,
Every pulse, a vibrant flow.
Luminous echoes call us near,
In the night, there's nothing to fear.

As we wander, hearts aglow,
Through the dreams of long ago.
An odyssey that knows no end,
In every star, a timeless friend.

Reverie in a Forest Dream

Whispers float through ancient trees,
A melody the heart believes.
In dappled light, shadows play,
Nature's tune leads me away.

Soft moss carpets the winding trail,
Each step sings a timeless tale.
Sunbeams dance on leaves so bright,
In this realm, the soul takes flight.

Crickets chirp a nighttime song,
In perfect peace, where I belong.
The air is thick with fragrant pine,
In this forest, all is divine.

Luminescence of Nature's Veil

Moonlight spills on dewy grass,
Glistening gems as shadows pass.
Each petal glows with silken hue,
Nature's art, a wondrous view.

Branches sway in gentle breeze,
Whispers soft as autumn leaves.
Radiance drapes the sleeping ground,
In this stillness, magic's found.

Stars adorn the velvet skies,
Where dreams emerge and softly rise.
Nature's light, a tender guide,
In the dark, we will abide.

Starlit Serenity in an Emerald Realm

Beneath the night, a world so bright,
Emerald leaves catch silver light.
The silence hums, a soothing balm,
In starlit dreams, I find my calm.

Crickets serenade the night air,
While moonbeams weave through branches rare.
Lost in wonder, I gently roam,
In this realm, I feel at home.

Mystic shadows, soft and deep,
Guard the secrets that trees keep.
In every breath, the magic swirls,
In nature's arms, my heart unfurls.

Fables Told by Flickering Fireflies

In twilight's glow, they come alive,
Tiny sparks in the night sky thrive.
With gentle light, they weave a tale,
Of whispered legends on the gale.

Dancing softly, they flit about,
Casting shadows, filling with doubt.
Each flicker holds a story sweet,
In the dark, where memories meet.

The forest listens, sighs in peace,
As tales of wonder never cease.
Fables told in a sparkling spree,
By fireflies, wild and free.

Glowing Heartbeats of Ancient Trees

In the stillness of the night,
Whispers drift through leaves so bright.
Roots entwined in secrets deep,
Ancient dreams in silence keep.

Gnarled trunks that bear the time,
With stories etched, a silent rhyme.
Branches sway, a gentle dance,
Embracing all in nature's trance.

Moonlight kisses every bark,
Calling forth the night's sweet spark.
In their shadows, spirits roam,
Glowing heartbeats find their home.

Beneath the stars, a sacred bond,
With every sigh, the world beyond.
Together they share sacred breath,
Life entwined, a dance with death.

Light Dripping from the Bracken

In the morning, dew drops gleam,
Catch the sunlight's golden beam.
Bracken sways with gentle grace,
Nature's art in every space.

Whispers float on soft, cool breeze,
Rustling whispers in the trees.
Golden hour brings the glow,
Life awakens, moving slow.

Fingers stretch to touch the light,
Chasing shadows, chasing bright.
Around each bend, the world unfolds,
Mysteries in green and golds.

Through the bracken, steps are light,
Dancing shadows blend with bright.
With each heartbeat, every spark,
Nature sings from dawn till dark.

Enchantment in Every Fluttering Leaf

In the breeze, they twist and twirl,
Nature's whispers softly swirl.
Colors blend in joyful dance,
Life's sweet hymn, a fleeting chance.

Each leaf tells a tale untold,
Crimson, gold, and shades of bold.
Flutter gently in the air,
Secrets woven, everywhere.

Sunlight filters through the shade,
Casting dreams in glimmers played.
In quiet moments, hearts can hear,
Enchanting echoes, crystal clear.

From the canopy above,
Rustling leaves share tales of love.
In every flutter, magic weaves,
Awakening the soul who believes.

Daybreak's Kiss on Woodland Creatures

As dawn awakens with a sigh,
Woodland creatures greet the sky.
Softly stretching, yawning wide,
Nature's wonder, morning's pride.

Deer bound lightly through the glade,
In the light, their secrets laid.
Rabbits dash, with playful glee,
Springing forth, wild and free.

Birds begin to sing their tune,
Melodies greet the warming moon.
Voices blend in harmonized cheer,
Echoing what hearts hold dear.

Daybreak's kiss on fur and feather,
Brings them closer, binds together.
In the woods, where dreams take flight,
Every creature feels the light.

Flickers of Gold in the Green

In the dappled shade, shadows play,
Flickering hues as sunlight sways.
A whisper of warmth in the cool air,
Golden sparks dance without a care.

Leaves rustle gently, nature's song,
In this moment, nothing feels wrong.
Life in the branches, a soft delight,
Flickers of gold, oh, such a sight.

Among the trunks where silence stands,
The gentle touch of nature's hands.
Each flicker beckons, a warm embrace,
In the green expanse, I find my place.

As night approaches, the glow stays near,
A memory held, crystal clear.
Flickers of gold in the fading light,
A promise of dawn, shining bright.

The Aglow of Sylvan Stories

Under the trees where secrets weave,
Aglow with tales the leaves believe.
Each rustle, a whisper from the past,
In sylvan realms, dreams are cast.

Moonlight spills through the branches wide,
With every shadow, my thoughts reside.
Stories of love, of loss, and grace,
Aglow in the stillness, time finds its pace.

The forest breathes in a timeless way,
Echoing laughter from a bygone day.
Each moment captured, pure delight,
In this aglow, my soul takes flight.

As dawn breaks softly, shadows fade,
Whispers of stories in memories laid.
The aglow remains, a tender thread,
Binding the heart to what lies ahead.

Murmurings of a Brightened Dawn

In the hush of night, when dreams take flight,
Murmurings rise with the approaching light.
A chorus of colors, the sky's embrace,
As dawn unfolds in a gentle pace.

The world awakens, painted anew,
With whispers of hope in the morning dew.
Each note a promise, each ray a song,
In the brightened dawn, we all belong.

Birds chatter sweetly, a joyful thrill,
Nature's orchestration on the hill.
Murmurings float in the crisp, clear air,
A symphony of life, beyond compare.

As the sun ascends, shadows grow pale,
In every heartbeat, a vibrant tale.
Murmurings linger, forever drawn,
In the light of day, we greet the dawn.

Sparkling Dewdrops on Fragile Petals

Morning light casts a glimmering hue,
Sparkling dewdrops on petals so new.
Each droplet dances, a crystal thread,
Softly embracing what nature has spread.

The flowers awaken, in colors bright,
In fragrant whispers, they greet the light.
Sparkling jewels on delicate grace,
A moment of beauty that time can't erase.

Among the blossoms, life starts to thrill,
With each gentle breeze, hearts are still.
Dewdrops like diamonds, on soft silk rest,
Nature's pure magic, at its best.

As the sun rises, shadows will flee,
Fragile petals sway, wild and free.
Sparkling moments in the soft dawn's glow,
Remind us of secrets the flowers know.

Whispers of Luminescent Leaves

In twilight's hush, the leaves do glow,
Soft whispers dance on breezes slow.
Each glimmer tells a tale of night,
As stars awaken, silver bright.

A canopy where secrets play,
In gentle hues, they fade away.
Nature's laughter, a sweet refrain,
In luminescence, joy remains.

Under the moon, the shadows twirl,
With every spin, the dreams unfurl.
Beneath the trees, a magic seen,
In whispers soft, the world feels keen.

Hold tight the moments, let them gleam,
For in the night, we drift and dream.
With every rustle, life takes flight,
In whispers of the purest light.

Shadows Dance Beneath the Canopy

Beneath the leaves, where shadows loom,
A silent waltz dispels the gloom.
The branches sway, a gentle sway,
In twilight's grasp, they find their play.

The forest breathes, a heartbeat near,
Each whisper echoes, pure and clear.
With every step, the echoes fade,
In secret paths, our dreams are laid.

Moonbeams peek through gaps above,
Illuminating all we love.
As shadows twine and softly blend,
Each fleeting moment feels like friend.

In this embrace of dark and light,
We find the magic of the night.
For in the dance of leaf and shade,
A timeless story we have made.

Enchanted Realms of Light

In realms where light and soft winds meet,
A magic stirs beneath our feet.
With every step, new wonders bloom,
In hidden paths, dispelling gloom.

The sunbeams filter through the trees,
In golden strands, we feel the breeze.
An orchestra of rustling leaves,
A song of life that never leaves.

With every flicker, colors rise,
Painting dreams across the skies.
These enchanted realms, they come alive,
Where hopes and wishes freely thrive.

Transforming shadows into grace,
In every turn, a warm embrace.
With open hearts, we chase the light,
In realms of wonder, pure delight.

Secrets Among the Foliage

Hidden whispers, soft and low,
Secrets shared where wild things grow.
Among the leaves, the stories weave,
In shadows deep, we dare believe.

The rustling tales, they intertwine,
With every flicker, each design.
A symphony of nature's tune,
Beneath the watchful eyes of moon.

Each leaf a page, each branch a road,
Leading us where dreams are sowed.
In emerald cloaks, the magic hides,
In quiet corners, love abides.

So let us wander, hand in hand,
In this lush and secret land.
Together we will find the key,
To all the tales of mystery.

Luminous Shadows Among the Pines

In twilight's glow, the shadows play,
Beneath tall pines where night meets day.
Soft whispers float on gentle breeze,
Among the boughs, the heart finds ease.

The starlit sky peeks through the leaves,
A canvas painted, nature weaves.
The echo of a distant call,
In tranquil woods, we lose our all.

Echoes of Forgotten Glades

In hidden glades where silence dwells,
Time lingers softly, weaving spells.
A memory stirs in the still air,
Of laughter lost, yet still we care.

The rustling leaves tell tales of old,
Of dreams once bright, now woven gold.
Beneath the arches of ancient trees,
We find our peace, our soul's release.

The Light that Kisses the Foliage

Through emerald leaves, the sunlight streams,
A golden touch on nature's dreams.
Each ray a whisper, soft and sweet,
Awakens life where shadows meet.

The floral scents rise from the ground,
In radiant hues, our joys abound.
Each moment glows, a fleeting kiss,
In every leaf, a glimpse of bliss.

Glistening Paths Through Whispering Trees

On winding paths, the light will dance,
Inviting hearts to take a chance.
With every step, the stories flow,
In every rustle, secrets grow.

The branches creak with ancient lore,
As shadows stretch and spirits soar.
Through whispered words of nature's tongue,
We find the songs that once were sung.

Whispers of Enchanted Leaves

In the breeze, the leaves confide,
Softly swaying, side to side.
They tell tales of nights gone past,
Of shadows, secrets, deep and vast.

Moonlight drips like silver dew,
Igniting dreams, making them true.
The forest hums a lullaby,
As ancient spirits softly sigh.

Each rustle speaks of love and loss,
Beneath the branches, mossy gloss.
The winds begin their gentle tease,
A dance amongst the whispered trees.

Nature's voice, a soothing balm,
In this haven, feeling calm.
With every step, I feel alive,
In whispers, mysteries thrive.

Radiance Beneath the Canopy

Sunbeams filter through the green,
A vibrant dance, a gentle sheen.
Leaves flutter down like soft confetti,
Nature's glory, ever ready.

In shadows deep, the creatures play,
Their laughter brightens up the day.
Flowers bloom with colors bold,
Painted stories waiting to be told.

Beeflies dart in sunlight's glow,
A fleeting moment, fast they go.
Each petal glimmers, softly bright,
A symphony of pure delight.

Here, time slows, the heart takes flight,
In the warmth of pure daylight.
Embrace the peace that nature weaves,
In radiance beneath the leaves.

Secrets in the Sunlit Glade

In a glade where wildflowers sway,
The sun spills gold at end of day.
Whispers echo among the trees,
Secrets carried on the breeze.

Beneath the sky, so vast and blue,
Nature's canvas, rich and true.
Creatures gather, play and prance,
In this world, they twirl and dance.

Mossy stones, a tranquil throne,
Where stories linger, softly grown.
A place of peace, a sacred space,
Bathed in sunlight's warm embrace.

Here lies wisdom, ancient lore,
In every corner, more and more.
The glade holds secrets deep and wide,
Where the heart and soul abide.

Twilight Dances in the Thicket

As twilight falls, the thicket stirs,
A ballet of shadows, a soft purr.
Fireflies sparkle, stars take flight,
A symphony of joy each night.

Underneath the velvet sky,
Whispers float as night winds sigh.
The branches sway, the critters tread,
In dreams where magic dances spread.

Each moment lingers, soft and sweet,
A heartbeat in this nightly feat.
The world transforms in dusk's embrace,
A hidden harmony, a secret place.

In the thicket, dreams unite,
With stars above, a wondrous sight.
In twilight's arms, we find our song,
Where we truly all belong.

Veils of Soft Starlight

In the hush of the night, skies unfold,
Whispers of dreams in silver and gold.
Shadows dance gently, a ballet of light,
Veils of starlight drape all in sight.

Moonbeams weave tales of magic unseen,
Sparkling like jewels on velvet of green.
Each glimmer a promise, a wish to believe,
In the quiet of darkness, our hearts can cleave.

The night birds serenade in a soft, lilted tone,
While shadows cascade like whispers alone.
Each flicker a journey, a path to explore,
Veils of starlight beckon, forever more.

A tapestry woven where silence prevails,
Dancing with echoes, where starlight sails.
Wrapped in the wonder, we glide and we weave,
In the magic of night, we learn how to believe.

The Luminous Heart of Nature

Deep in the wild where wonders play,
Nature's heart beats night and day.
Sunlight glimmers on leaves so bright,
In the canopy's embrace, pure delight.

Streams whisper softly through rocks and moss,
Echoing secrets, never a loss.
Every petal and leaf tells a tale,
Of the forest's embrace, of its gentle veil.

Colors collide in a vibrant song,
Where the melodies of life glow strong.
The luminous heart, so vast and wide,
Welcomes all souls, a nurturing guide.

In the arms of the trees, we find our peace,
In the rustling leaves, all worries cease.
Nature's soft heartbeat, a calming grace,
In its luminous heart, we find our place.

Crystals in the Underbrush

In the tangled thicket where wildflowers bloom,
Crystals lie hidden, dispelling the gloom.
Glistening softly beneath mossy beds,
Whispers of earth in their silence spreads.

Each stone holds a story, a dance of the earth,
Twenty million years of magic and birth.
Shimmering softly, the colors collide,
Crystals in shadows, where secrets reside.

The light filters down through the canopy green,
Awakening beauty in places unseen.
Fragments of wonder, like dreams set free,
Crystals in underbrush, beckoning me.

Each step in the forest uncovers more clues,
Mysteries tangled in nature's deep hues.
The treasure of moments where stillness is found,
Crystals in the underbrush, magic unbound.

Dreamscapes in the Forest's Embrace

Beneath the tall trees where shadows entwine,
Dreamscapes awaken, a world so divine.
Misty and soft, the landscape unfolds,
In the hush of the forest, a story is told.

Whispers of fables, the breeze carries bright,
Every rustle and sigh is a promise of light.
The realm of the fairies, the songs of the night,
In dreamscapes of wonder, our spirits take flight.

Golden dappled sunlight spills through the leaves,
Painting illusions that the heart believes.
Blossoms like laughter, in colors that gleam,
Awake in the forest, lost in a dream.

So wander, dear heart, where the wildflowers sway,
In the forest's embrace, let your worries decay.
Dreamscapes await in each shimmering space,
Here in the stillness, find your true place.

Radiant Trails of Silvery Mist

In dawn's embrace, whispers flow,
Radiant trails where soft winds blow.
Silvery hues light up the day,
Nature's magic on display.

Through meadows lush, the mist shall glide,
Painting dreams where shadows hide.
Each step beckons, secrets call,
In the silence, we feel small.

A gentle touch on leaves so green,
In this moment, all unseen.
The world awakes with song and breath,
In the stillness, we find depth.

With every swirl, a tale unfolds,
Of ancient woods and hearts so bold.
Radiant trails in softest light,
Guide us onward, day and night.

Echoes of Nightfall's Glow

As twilight drapes the earth in grace,
Echoes whisper in this space.
Stars awaken in darkened skies,
Casting dreams where silence lies.

The moon, a lantern, softly beams,
Shimmering bright on silver streams.
Each shadow dances, time stands still,
In the coolness, hearts can fill.

Crickets sing their nightly tune,
While fireflies flicker, seeking moon.
In this magic, we find peace,
As worries fade and tensions cease.

Echoes linger in the breeze,
Carrying secrets through the trees.
Nightfall's glow, a tender sight,
Guides us gently into night.

Twinkling Gaze of Ancient Trees

In forest depths where ancients stand,
Gaze reveals a timeless land.
Twinkling leaves in gentle sway,
Guard the stories of the day.

Roots entwined in silent trust,
With each season, grow we must.
Branches reach for skies above,
In their presence, feel the love.

Whispers echo through the boughs,
Tales of strength, of silent vows.
Underneath their watchful eyes,
In the shadows, wisdom lies.

Twinkling gaze, a guiding light,
In dark places, gives us sight.
With every step, we feel it there,
Ancient trees and timeless air.

A Symphony of Shimmering Branches

Under canopies where dreams reside,
A symphony begins to slide.
Shimmering branches sway and flow,
In harmony, their secrets grow.

Leaves flutter like soft, whispered notes,
Carried gently, time emotes.
Nature's chorus, rich and sweet,
In the stillness, hearts can meet.

The breeze conducts with tender care,
As sunlight weaves through secret air.
Dappled shadows dance in the light,
Creating magic, pure delight.

A symphony, oh how it soars,
In this world, our spirit roars.
Shimmering branches reach for the skies,
Playing songs that never die.

A Tapestry of Light and Leaf

Sunlight dapples through the trees,
Crafting shadows on the ground.
Every leaf a delicate art,
In nature's gallery, profound.

Whispers rustle in the air,
As branches dance with gentle ease.
Life unfolds in vibrant hues,
A symphony of rustling leaves.

Each moment holds a vivid hue,
Colors blend, a painter's dream.
Nature weaves a tapestry,
In every stitch, a shared theme.

With whispers soft, the forest breathes,
Embroidered by the hands of time.
A dance of light, a leaf's embrace,
In this haven, life's sweet rhyme.

Phosphorescent Whispers of the Wild

In twilight's grasp, the world ignites,
Glowing trails of firefly flight.
Nature speaks in glowing tones,
A symphony of whispered light.

Beneath the stars, shadows play,
With creatures stirring in the night.
Every leaf a glimmering spark,
In darkness, they shine so bright.

Mossy carpets cradle dreams,
As wildflowers sway and gleam.
Echoes of life rustle so,
Nature's whispers, a gentle theme.

In the stillness, secrets pulse,
Night's breath lingers, wild and free.
A phosphorescent serenade,
In this wild symphony we see.

Beneath Canopies of Celestial Glow

Stars peek through the leafy veil,
Their glimmer soft, a gentle sigh.
Beneath this dome of twinkling light,
The universe sings, and we comply.

Branches cradle the night's embrace,
While shadows weave through ancient trees.
A cosmic dance, serene and slow,
In nature's hold, our hearts take ease.

The air is heavy with dreams untold,
As constellations guide our way.
A tapestry of light above,
Inviting hope at the end of day.

In silence deep, with hearts aglow,
Beneath this roof of endless night.
We leave behind our cares and woes,
In the cosmos, we find our light.

Moonlit Murmurs in the Underbrush

A silver sheen upon the ground,
As moonlight weaves through tangled fern.
In whispers soft, the night resounds,
While dreams and shadows twist and turn.

Creatures stir in the quiet dark,
Their secrets held beneath the trees.
The night is cloaked in softest veils,
Where every rustle hints at peace.

The world lies hushed in moonlit grace,
As if the earth itself holds breath.
In hidden corners, magic blooms,
Each heartbeat echoes life, not death.

Here in the midst of woven night,
The wilderness shares its ancient lore.
With every murmur, every sigh,
The earth whispers tales forevermore.

Glistening Dreams Beneath the Stars

In the quiet of night,
Soft whispers take flight.
Glimmers of hope shine bright,
Chasing shadows out of sight.

Stars twinkle like fire,
Igniting deepest desire.
With every wish we send,
Glistening dreams never end.

Beneath this vast expanse,
We find our hearts in trance.
Floating on moonlit streams,
We wander through our dreams.

In the silence we share,
Our thoughts float in the air.
A canvas painted light,
Glistening dreams hold tight.

Glow of Forgotten Tales

In dusty books we find,
Stories left behind.
With each turn of the page,
Ghosts softly engage.

Whispers in the dark,
Flicker like a spark.
From shadows they arise,
Under ancient skies.

They dance on faded lines,
Of love and lost designs.
Recalling every thrill,
With a haunting chill.

In the glow of the past,
These moments hold fast.
Forgotten tales revive,
In memories, we thrive.

A Tapestry of Radiance

Threads of gold entwined,
In patterns so refined.
Each hue a story starts,
Woven through our hearts.

Colors blend and merge,
As passions start to surge.
Dancing in the light,
Creating pure delight.

Whispers of the loom,
Fill the air with bloom.
A tapestry unfolds,
With wonders to be told.

In every woven strand,
Magic seems to stand.
A canvas of our dreams,
In radiant beams.

Splendor in the Shifting Shadows

As daylight starts to fade,
New wonders are displayed.
Shadows stretch and creep,
Secrets in silence keep.

In twilight's gentle hold,
Stories softly told.
A world of wonder grows,
Where mystery bestows.

Dancing figures twirl,
In a vibrant swirl.
With each night that falls,
Enchanting darkness calls.

In sudden bursts of light,
Splendor ignites the night.
Eclipses of desire,
Flame the heart's wild fire.

The Soundtrack of Glittering Time

In whispers of wind that softly flow,
Time dances lightly, a gentle show.
Moments like notes, sweetly entwined,
Echoes of laughter, a melody signed.

Under the stars, the shadows play,
Each tick of the clock, a bright display.
Memories twinkle, in silver and gold,
A symphony crafted, a story retold.

The heartbeat of life, rhythmic and true,
Waves of the past, forever in view.
In every sigh, a tale to share,
In the soundtrack of time, we find our care.

So listen closely, as moments rhyme,
For every heartbeat is a cherished chime.
In the orchestra of dreams, let us thrive,
With the soundtrack of glittering time, we arrive.

Luminescence Beneath the Twilight

As daylight fades to a whispering glow,
The stars awaken, in evening's flow.
Soft beams dance on the leaves so fair,
A tranquil light spreads, beyond compare.

Beneath the twilight, secrets arise,
In the coolness, the world complies.
Each spark that flickers, a flick of fate,
Illuminates dreams as we contemplate.

Gentle breezes carry sweetly sung,
Echoes of stories, forever young.
In the hush between silence and night,
Luminescence glimmers, our hearts ignite.

So let us wander, through shadows deep,
In twilight's embrace, where secrets keep.
With every breath, the stars align,
In the dance of dusk, we find our sign.

Star-Dusted Ferns

In wooded realms where whispers dwell,
Star-dusted ferns have tales to tell.
Each leaf a canvas, each frond a dream,
Bathed in starlight, they shimmer and gleam.

Among the trees, in shadows they play,
Guarding the magic of night and day.
They sway with grace in the moon's embrace,
A delicate tapestry, nature's lace.

With glimmers of silver on emerald bright,
They breathe in darkness, exhale the light.
Each rustle a secret, each bend a sign,
In the glow of the cosmos, they intertwine.

So stroll through the woods where the ferns reside,
In the heart of the forest, let wonder guide.
For within their rustling, beauty transcends,
In the lore of the ferns, the universe bends.

Secrets of the Charmed Glade

In a hidden glade where magic flows,
Whispers of nature in soft undertows.
Sunlight dapples the ground so sweet,
Where wildflowers gather, our hearts meet.

Branches knit overhead in a gentle embrace,
The breeze carries echoes, a warm, safe space.
Every step forward, a soft, sacred vow,
As the secrets unfold, we ponder the how.

With each turn of leaf, a story in bloom,
In the charm of the glade, we banish all gloom.
The heart of the forest beats steady and true,
In the stillness, we find what we always knew.

So linger awhile, let stillness prevail,
In the depths of the glade, magic will sail.
For the secrets held dear in nature's hand,
Are the whispers of life, forever we stand.

Milton Keynes UK
Ingram Content Group UK Ltd.
UKHW021949151124
451186UK00007B/169